Freedom
Copyright © 2018 by Robert Rice

All rights reserved. No part of this publication may be reproduced, distributed, or transmitted in any form or by any means, including photocopying, recording, or other electronic or mechanical methods, without the prior written permission of the author, except in the case of brief quotations embodied in critical reviews and certain other non-commercial uses permitted by copyright law.

Tellwell Talent
www.tellwell.ca

ISBN
978-0-2288-0444-4 (Hardcover)
978-0-2288-0443-7 (Paperback)
978-0-2288-0445-1 (eBook)

freedom

FREEDOM

Life has humans the author of their own destiny with natural evolution in clean slate with the ability and freedom at the creation of one's own engagement in the evolution of living. Instead of qualifying a human being with concept such as faults and qualities which he or she inherited at birth a human being is born with potentiality at becoming a person he or she chooses to be. I am not referring here to choice of profession or trade which surely refers to aptitudes but to the quality of one's life.

> No one is born hating another person because of the colour of his skin or religion. People must learn to hate, and if they can learn to hate, they can be taught to love, for love comes more naturally to the human heart than its opposite."
>
> - Nelson MENDELLA

Then people brought little children to Jesus for him to place his hands on them and pray for them but the disciples rebuked them: Jesus said, "let the little children come to me, and do not hinder them, for the kingdom of heaven belongs to such as these." at that time the disciples came to Jesus and asked, "who, then, is the greatest in the kingdom of heaven? "He called a little child to him, and placed the child among them. And he said: "Truly I tell you, unless you change and become like little children, you will never enter the kingdom of heaven. Therefore, whoever takes the lowly position of this child is the greatest in the kingdom of heaven and whoever welcomes one such child in my name welcomes me.

- Matthew 19:13-15 new international version (niv)

Several influences in a child's early life may have disrupted its natural evolution. One may achieve this by becoming aware of the several hindrances that may have either prevented or impeded its self-actualization. We start by emphasizing that we came into this world with a clean slate, without preconceptions or prejudices. I am aware of some religious teaching that state the opposite and at one time I believed it was so.

I have reached an altogether conclusion after these several years as a jurist and generally as an inquisitive human. I believe people are born with good dispositions. Family and surrounding values exerts substantial influence on a child's insight and perception such as a learning bent on establishing a belief or a way of life to repress a child's candid ability of creation and spontaneity.

> *Knowing why one holds a belief does not necessarily bring knowledge. A belief is a belief because it is not knowledge. Unfortunately, every individual's upbringing helps invest him with a set of beliefs which, adopted when too young to be questioned, often come to masquerade as knowledge.*

> *According to Hans Toch, the eloquent and insightful author of 'The social psychology of social movements', the combined effect of child indoctrination and the socialization process, at its most successful and effective level serves to blinker an individual to reality and create dependence on a belief system any belief system. He can take blacks or whites but not the shifting shades in between. Indoctrination is an emotive word. Perhaps for most people it is most commonly associated with the rather blatant process of persuasion that goes on in totalitarian regimes the systematize thinking encouraged in minority political groups or religious cults (that other people belong to) where slogans or catchwords, such as 'state control' or 'enlightenment' encapsulate central*

concepts. It has a bad flavour, feel, implying that the indoctrinated person has taken on board the conclusions of others instead of coming to his or her own. It flies in the face of free thinking, the rational weighing up of argument and all such ideals that we think we hold dear.

- The manipulated mind- Denise winn 1983 page 37.Malor books 2000)
<u>*Unquestioned Belief*</u>*

George Bernard Shaw: There is nothing that can be changed more completely than human nature when the job is taken in hand early enough >. (STEVEN PINKER Blank slate p.288

AT SHAKESPEARE PHILOSOPHY/COLIN McQUINN 2006 PAGE13-14 on *Causality,* spontaneity and creativity is suppressed and life is preordained. This is a rational view. I was raised on a farm and this treatise reminds me of the head gear of a horse which was made for the horse to see only in one direction with no peripheral access. This is living with a set of rules established through indoctrination at a young age. This is God's will they said. Living consist of utilising a set of established events or the application of guidelines; such is a dead world with no surprises nor creativity nor spontaneity; humans are like trees with a rigid agenda of which they have no control;

> How does the world work? What governs the flow of events? One thing gives rise to another and so on indefinitely; but what principles lie behind this causal unfolding? What How does the world work? What governs the flow of events? Thing gives rise to another, generating yet another, and so on indefinitely; but what principles lie behind this causal unfolding? What explains the causal sequence of the universe? There is a reason for what happens, even if it may be inscrutable: events are planned, designed a certain way, with foresight of some sort. One view is that a rational intelligence organizes the causal relations that characterize the way the world evolves-as it might be, the

Christian God. Whenever one thing brings about another you can ask what explains this causality and expect there to be an answer in rational terms it was in order that something be so. The world is an intelligible place and causal relationships manifest that intelligibility. The universe is like a clock designed by a supreme intelligence: everything in it has a place, a function, and the whole has a purpose. According to this type of view, it is generally assumed that there is an ethical purpose behind what happens: some sort of cosmic justice controls the sequence of events, so that things happen "for the best:' If a battle is won by a particular side, it was because the universe intended it; it was part of a large cosmic plan, an instance of divine justice. This view is naturally associated with the conviction that the universe was created by an intelligent and just God, and He imprinted His nature on the world. He may work in mysterious ways, but He is always manifest that intelligibility good in mind. Causality is never blind, always purposeful. Death itself is a part of this rational plan there is a reason to what happens, a meaning. Clearly, it goes along with a theistic view of the universe. In its simplest formulation, it holds that causation is moral: what actually happens ought to happen.

Set against this teleological view, we have the conception generally associated with the eighteenth-century skeptical philosopher David Hume, that causation is simply brute temporal sequence, with nothing rational underwriting it at all. No rational principle connects a cause to its effect, according to Hume; causation does not have its basis in reason at all. As it is sometimes put, causation is just one damn thing after another-merely the conjunction of intrinsically unrelated events. There is no meaning to any of it; it is simply nature blindly following whatever laws govern it, with a large dose of randomness thrown in. Hume was an atheist and his view of causation fits that world view perfectly: nothing confers meaning or rationality on causation; the process is essentially mindless. In principle, anything can cause anything-it is just a matter of what actually happens in nature, not some preconceived ideal of intelligible order. Rationality belongs only in human minds, and that to a limited degree; there is no rationality in nature itself. A person's death, say, is not the unfolding of a divine plan, but a mindless event not different in kind from any other instance of causation-a raindrop falling, the sun setting. In particular, causation is morally neutral a purpose: there is no cosmic justice governing the way causation works out, no redeeming explanation of apparent catastrophe. Right and wrong exercise no hold over causation whatsoever. Morality comes only from rational agents; it has nothing to do with the course of nature considered in itself.

* * *

How can there be a genuine personal action sprung from a private and exclusive assessment unless the person is free to choose values unhampered by principles and standards. It is one thing to know of teachings and precepts which may very well be accepted after assessment and one copied from tutored values. This is like applying a blueprint of life acknowledging one's inability at creating one. The message here is to reach a decision from one's own evaluation. Steve Jobs demonstrate why certain education could have a harmful impact:

The wisdom of Steve Jobs

"Your time is limited, so don't waste it living someone else's life. Don't be trapped by dogma which is living with the results of other people's thinking. Don't let the noise of others' opinions drown out your own inner voice. And most important, have the courage to follow your heart and intuition." Steve Job (w20 Most Memorable Quotes From Steve Jobs - The Cheat Sheet www.cheatsheet.com/mon

A perspective of life has humans the author of their own destiny with life evolving with their participations. It recognizes that one is native of a clean slate with the ability and freedom at the creation of one's own engagement in the evolution of living.

Henri Bergson (1859–1941) was a famous and influential French philosophers of the late 19th century-early 20th century.

1. Life and works

Bergson attempted to redefine the relations between science and metaphysics, intelligence and intuition, and insisted on the necessity of increasing thought's possibility through the use of intuition, which, according to him, alone approached a knowledge of the absolute and of real life, understood as pure duration. Because of his (relative) criticism of intelligence, he makes a frequent use of images and metaphors in his writings in order to avoid the use of concepts, which (he considers) fail to touch the whole of reality, being only a sort of abstract net thrown on things. For instance, he says in The Creative Evolution (chap.III) that thought in itself would never have thought it possible for the human being to swim, as it cannot deduce swimming from walking. For swimming to be possible, man must throw itself in water, and only then can thought consider swimming as possible. Intelligence, for Bergson, is a practical faculty rather than a pure speculative faculty, a product of evolution used by man to survive. If metaphysics is to avoid "false problems", it should not extend to pure speculation the abstract concepts of intelligence, but rather intuition.

- Creative evolution First published Tue May 18, 2004; substantive revision Mon Mar 21, 2016

In place of applying a rational method in resolving the issue of good and evil reliance on one's ability to discriminate is intuition. One just know!

Book Title

Robert D Richardson's book on Emmerson (THE MIND ON FIRE NOV 6, 1996) relate that Ralph Emmerson acknowledged Rousseau like convictions. He believed that we were born wholesome and open to the world and others.

> "Here you are in the universe, and so long as particular conditions obtain-food air, beauty, interest, the promise of adventure-you leap into existence. You show yourself in the way you organize the materials of your world: your ideas and feelings, body and relationships. You are not just the things you do, not just the thoughts you think, the convictions you hold you are that which shapes these. You are a power creating the whole complex work of art that is your life your manifestation in the world".

Nietzsche proclaimed that the god we were educated to accept was dead. He relied on the overflowing ability of humans to tailor their lives.

> Friedrich Nietzsche (1844–1900) was a German philosopher and cultural critic who published intensively in the 1870s and 1880s. He is famous for uncompromising criticisms of traditional European morality and religion, as well as of conventional philosophical ideas and social and political pieties associated with modernity. Many of these criticisms rely on psychological diagnoses that expose false consciousness infecting people's received ideas; for that reason, he is often associated with a group of late modern thinkers (including Marx and Freud) who advanced a "hermeneutics of suspicion" against traditional values (see Foucault [1964] 1990, Ricoeur [1965] 1970, Leiter 2004). Nietzsche also used his psychological analyses to support original theories about the nature of the self and provocative proposals suggesting new values that he thought would promote cultural renewal and improve social and psychological life by

comparison to life under the traditional values he criticized. Following is a summary of his thoughts:

The individual is a law unto himself, unpredictable and unmanageable. Society, then, cannot be composed of individuals. It requires members. Man must be made "uniform"and o'calculable"; for this purpose morality and the"social straitjacket" are employed. The purpose of establishing society and its fiction of mankind, Nietzsche contended, was to prevent people from becoming individuals, to make them "common" (GW 10:400). The price of social membership is the forfeiture of self-rule, this by means of establishing social norms: "Through his morality the individual outvotes himself' (HH 232).-"The objective of all human arrangements is through distracting one's thoughts to cease to be aware of life. Why does the great man desire the opposite-to be aware precisely of life that is to say to suffer from life-so strongly? Because he realizes that he is in danger of being cheated out of himself and that a kind of agreement exists to kidnap him out of his own cave. Then he bestirs himself, pricks up his ears, and resolves: 'I will remain my own!'(UM 154). Only the few are capable of such resolve. The majority remain happy in their masquerades...

- Stanford encyclopedia of philosophy march 17 2017

Søren Aabye Kierkegaard 5 May 1811/ 1 November 1855) was a Danish philosopher, theologian, poet, social critic and religious author who is widely considered to be the first existentialist philosopher. He wrote critical texts on organized religion, Christendom, morality, ethics, psychology, and the philosophy of religion, displaying a fondness for metaphor, irony and parables. Much of his philosophical work deals with the issues of how one lives as a "single individual", giving priority to concrete human reality over abstract thinking and highlighting the importance of personal choice and commitment. He was against literary critics who defined idealist intellectuals and philosophers of his time..he emphasized above all the need to be come a true individual passionately committed to a path personally chosen likens real existence to riding a wild stallion as contrasted with fallen asleep on a moving hay wagon..

For Kierkegaard, man is essentially an individual, not a member of a species or race; and ethical and religious truth is known through individual existence and decision-through subjectivity, not objectivity. Systems of thought and a dialectic such as Hegel's are matters merely of thought, which cannot comprise individual existence and decision. Such systems leave out, said Kierkegaard, the unique and essential "spermatic point, the individual, ethically and religiously conceived, and existentially accentuated." Similarly in the works of the American author Henry David Thoureau, writing at the same time as Kierkegaard, there is an emphasis on the solitary individual as the bearer of ethical responsibility, who, when he is right, carries the preponderant ethical weight against the state, government, and a united public opinion, when they are wrong. The solitary individual with right on his side is always "a majority of one."

- Ethics, the study of moral values, by Mortimer J. Adler and Seymour Cain. Pref. by William Ernest Hocking. 1962 p. 252.

MONTAIGNE is the most significant philosophers of the French Renaissance, known for popularizing the essay as a literary genre. (Wikipedia) Born: February 28, 1533, Château de Montaigne, Saint-Michel-de-Montaigne, France Died: September 13, 1592, Here is one of his essays: Although written some four centuries ago Montaigne's observations are amazingly relevant today:

Montaigne, observing the world, is struck by one thing: few people are not themselves. Human beings live outside themselves. They do not say what they live, what they feel, what they think. They act according to others for fear of being alone or desire to please. This leads to a false form of discourse and behavior. Hence the reaction of Montaigne and the sense of his commitment to the ego. We do more for humanity and for truth by enunciating a thought that comes from itself than by posting opinions by conformity or seduction. The ego is above all an ethic. This is what gives it its reality. One is self-resisting to all conformism, beginning with individual conformity.

Montaigne expresses this spirit of resistance well when he writes: "It is enough lived for others, live for us at least this end of life." Let us bring our thoughts and our intentions to our ease. It is a good part of our retreat, but it prevents us, without interfering with others, since God gives us leisure to dispose of our engagement; Luggage; Let us take leave of the Company early; Let us dispatch ourselves of those violent attacks which engage us elsewhere, and take us away from us.

- INTERNET ENCYCLOPEDIA OF PHILOSOPHY

The political philosopher, Hannah Arendt (1906-1975), was born in Hanover, Germany, in 1906, the only child of secular Jews. During childhood, Arendt moved first to Konigsberg (East Prussia) and later to Berlin. In 1922-23, Arendt began her studies (in classics and Christian theology) at the University of Berlin, and in 1924 entered Marburg University, where she studied philosophy with Martin Heidegger. She wrote about people who simply copy others:

"those who do not think, who relies on other thoughts ideas and mandatory truths and merely being captive of the 'continuous flow of daily life" without curiosity or love for the beauty, wisdom, and justice and wisdom, these bury themselves in the abyss of futility and his spirit dies. But thinking is not the prerogative of certain human vocations even elected but the vocation of everyone: thinking and to reflect on the consequences of one' actions does not depend on the social, education or the intellectual value of the individuals."

Arendt points out that "wickedness can be caused by the absence of thought-".

"When that man abandons his human duty to think by laziness or often fear, he becomes prey to the worst Phantasmagoria. To turn down thinking is to choose sleepwalking and fit in the social and political need and forget the state that gives man the ability to carry on and be free." (Translation is mine)

Political judgement, and its crisis in the modern era, is a recurrent theme in her work. As noted earlier, Arendt bemoans the "world alienation" that characterizes Arendt's concern the modern era, the destruction of a stable institutional and experiential world that could provide a stable context in which humans could organize their collective existence. Moreover, it will be recalled that in human action Arendt recognizes (for good or ill) the capacity to bring the new, unexpected, and unanticipated into the world. This quality of action means that it constantly threatens to defy or exceed our existing categories of understanding or judgement; precedents and rules cannot help us judge properly what is unprecedented and new. So for Arendt, our categories and standards of thought are always beset by their potential inadequacy with respect to that which they are called upon to judge. However, this aporia of judgement reaches a crisis point in the 20th century under the repeated impact of its monstrous and unprecedented events. The mass destruction of two World Wars, the development of technologies which threaten global annihilation, the rise of totalitarianism, and the murder of millions in the Nazi death camps and Stalin's purges have effectively exploded our existing standards for moral and political judgement. Tradition lies in shattered fragments around us and "the very framework within which understanding and judging could arise is gone." The shared bases of understanding, handed down to us in our tradition, seem irretrievably lost.

Arendt confronts the question: on what basis can one judge the unprecedented, the incredible, the monstrous which defies our established understandings and experiences? If we are to judge at all, it must now be "without preconceived categories and…without the set of customary rules which is morality;" it must be "thinking without a bannister" In order to secure the possibility of such judgement Arendt must establish that there in fact exists "an independent human faculty, unsupported by law and public opinion, that judges anew in full spontaneity every deed and intent whenever the occasion arises." This for Arendt comes to represent "one of the central moral questions of all time, namely…the nature and function of human judgement." It is with this goal and this question in mind that the work of Arendt's final years converges on the "unwritten political philosophy" of Kant's Critique of Judgement.

The fundamental defining quality of action is its in eliminable freedom, its status as an end in itself and so as subordinate to nothing outside itself.

Our sense of an inner freedom is derivative upon first having experienced "a condition of being free as a tangible worldly reality. We first become aware of freedom or its opposite in our intercourse with others, not in the intercourse with ourselves." In defining action as freedom, and freedom as action, we can see the decisive influence of Augustine upon Arendt's thought. From Augustine's political philosophy (ST Augustine) she takes the theme of human action as beginning:

To act, in its most general sense, means to take initiative, to begin (as the Greek word archein, 'to begin,' 'to lead,' and eventually 'to rule' indicates), to set something in motion. Because they are initium, newcomers and beginners by virtue of birth, men take initiative, are prompted into action.

And further, that freedom is to be seen as a character of human existence in the world. Man does not so much possess freedom as he, or better his coming into the world, is equated with the appearance of freedom in the universe; man is free because he is a beginning...

In short, humanity represents/articulates/embodies the faculty of beginning. It follows from this equation of freedom, action and beginning that freedom is "an accessory of doing and acting;" "Men are free...as long as they act, neither before nor after; for to be free and to act are the same." This capacity for initiation gives actions the character of singularity and uniqueness, as "it is in the nature of beginning that something new is started which cannot be expected from whatever happened before." So, intrinsic to the human capacity for action is the introduction of genuine novelty, the unexpected, unanticipated and unpredictable into the world: The new always happens against the overwhelming odds of statistical laws and their probability, which for all practical, everyday purposes amounts to certainty; the new therefore always appears in the guise of a miracle.

- POLITIQUE ER PENSÉE PETITE BLIOTHÈQUE PAYOT PAGE 351 (2004 Éditions payot et Rivarges)

IF THE ENDS ARE THE ENDS OF OUR NATURES,WE ARE AS SPINOSA CONSTANTLY POINTS OUT, FREE. Only when we are subject to alien ends or the ends of alien natures are we enslaves. For freedom is not opposed to determinism... but in complete self-determination.

(the philosophy of spinosa-Joseph Ratner-1927 The courage and wisdom of this remarkable person contributed greatly to the emancipation of humankind particularly in exposing the several myths in the Bible.

You are good when you are one with yourself 'KAHLIL GIBRAN

Freedom has to do with becoming or being what we are as individuals not as a group although our manners, jobs and taste share common characteristics to our milieu we nonetheless are unique and different in various ways from other members of our group. If freedom is reached partly or wholly when we attain that which make us unique it follows that indiscriminate conformity to values and norms extrinsic to our real self may become a serious obstacle to the attainment of this goal.

It is one thing to know of teachings and precepts and another to be restricted by them in one's preferences and alternatives. Unless each action or decision is treated as a new experience requiring as well a novel decision there is an unstructured or unplanned act. We are relentlessly and unconsciously mandated to apply tutored values without question. Self- reliance is something of a sin. It is easier to copy others and not fret about becoming one-self .

Real and true living has to do with one's fleeting evaluation of the path or actions one chooses at each moments of life. That choice is very much a personal one and is made with the assurance of one' spontaneity to make the best decision instead of engaging in the postulation of past sayings, truism. That requires a development of one' ability to become his or her real self. Some community establishes their values and custom as being the proper demeanour shunning basic wants which are either performed in concealment or at other communities. One is not to show their true self but a facial expression akin to the false posture he wishes to convey. Hypocrisy becomes a virtue.

In 'Being and nothingness' the philosopher Jean-Paul SARTRE (partially of Protestant origin) writes about being true as

Opposed to performing a function.

For Sartre, the spirit of seriousness would be attached to the dogmatic religious, who decreed that moral values pre-exist the man. Equivalent of bad faith in the moral field, the spirit of serious would be the opposite of existential freedom that the human being must conquer by building its own values:

> The 'serious' man is one who think himself as president of his business, as dignitary of the Legion of honour, as Member of the faculty, but also as a father, as husband, or any other half, mi-social function. Because, in being so, he identifies willingly in an arbitrary function which he is indebted to society. The spirit of seriousness is the outstanding denial of freedom, because it leads to man to the inevitable transformation that undergoes all humans when he merge in society. Everyone knows perfectly well in his true self that he cannot be identical to his function. The spirit of seriousness is the denial by excellence of freedom..... Since everyone knows perfectly well he can't be identical to its function.. the spirit of seriousness means bad faith in the sense of "undue pretension. Kafka showed in *America*, the ridiculous and the danger of this vain dignity which manifests itself in identifying himself to the office. In this novel, the person foremost trustworthy personnel of the hotel upon which depends the position and the daily bread of the hero, waived the possibility he could make a mistake by conjuring the argument of the serious man: "How could I continue to be super if I would confuse someone for another person?

> (I would refer to that person as someone who attempts to be someone else.)

Author Name

- INTERNET OF PHILOSOPHY (SARTE)

.Gilles Deleuze. A French philosopher in the laste 20th century observed in his works(as depicted by Arnaud Bouaniche 's Gilles Deleuze an introduction) that humans were able to free themselves from retraining impediments to their evolution:

"He claims that standards of value are internal or immanent: to live well is to fully express one's power, to go to the limits of one's potential, rather than to judge what exists by non-empirical, transcendent standards. Modern society still suppresses difference and alienates persons from what they can do. To affirm reality, which is a flux of change and difference, we must overturn established identities and so become all that we can become though we cannot know what that is in advance. The pinnacle of Deleuzean practice, then, is creativity. "Herein, perhaps, lies the secret: to bring into existence and not to judge.

- Essays Critical and Clinical, p. 135

This article appeared in a Canadian newspaper in 2016.

MONEY IS NOT HAPPINESS

In1958, Japan had an average per capita income of about $3,000. By 1989, Japan was one of the wealthiest nations in the world, but there had been little discernible change in subjective well being(a mere 3% increase over 30 years).You might protest that these figures are societal averages: Surely the most affluent members of society feel like they have enough? But I've spent 13 years as a certified financial planner, and my financial-planning firm, Abacus, works with many high- and ultrahigh-net-worth individuals and

I can tell you emphatically that money does not buy happiness. You might protest that these figures are societal averages: Surely the most affluent members of society feel like they have enough? But I've spent 13 years as a certified financial planner, and my financial-planning firm, Abacus, works with many high- and ultrahigh-net-worth individuals and I can tell you emphatically that money does not buy happiness. In fact, in a study of members of the Forbes 400 "richest" list, the world's wealthiest individuals rated their satisfaction at exactly the same level as did the Inuit people of northern Greenland and the Masai of Kenya, who have no electricity or running water

One has to learn to live in the instant to relish life. That can only occur if one's attention in thoughts is not of the past or the future but the present. Every moment ought to be a novel one otherwise one will repeat or apply a planned path.

Nowadays most are engage in a most occupying way with electronic gadgets so much so that there seem to be little time to get in touch with their feelings or inner self. This attraction appear to be in the domain of addictions inducing the person to escape from themselves. The New York Times in 2010 published an article on this topic:

> According to a June 7th, 2010 New York Times article ("Hooked On Gadgets and Paying A Mental Price"), our electronic gadgets, rather than freeing us, are contributing to stress and time pressures. The article talks about people who are "addicted" to their electronic devices, checking emails, texting, playing games and interacting on social networking sites. Their "addiction" has, in many cases, had a negative impact on their relationships, grades in school and health. The article describes how "One in 7 married respondents said the use of these devices was causing them to see less of their spouses. And 1 in 10 said they spent less time with their children under 10."
>
> The article quotes Dr. Kimberly Young, a professor at St. Bonaventure University in New York who has led research on

the addictive nature of online technology. Dr. Young suggests therapy for a person "addicted" to electronics to determine why a person needs to use these devices "as a way of escape. I suggest that therapy isn't needed to determine why a person uses these devices to escape. Escape is the whole point of these devices

www.ingramcontent.com/pod-product-compliance
Lightning Source LLC
LaVergne TN
LVHW020006080526
838200LV00081B/4472